VI to Shanghai
The Story of Feng-Shan Ho –
Chinese diplomat in Vienna who saved thousands of Jews during the Holocaust

Robert F. Holden
Illustrations by Joy Kolitsky

MARGATE, NEW JERSEY

Copyright © 2022 by Robert Holden
All rights reserved. No part of this book may be used or reproduced in any manner, electronic or mechanical, including photocopying, recording or by any information storage and retrieval system, or otherwise, without written permission from the publisher.

MARGATE, NEW JERSEY

A division of ComteQ Communications, LLC
609-487-9000
Email: publisher@ComteQpublishing.com

This book was made possible through the generous support of the British Columbia Association for Learning and Preserving the History of WW II in Asia (BC ALPHA).
Their slogan is:
"Show me, I'll remember; involve me, I'll understand."

ISBN 978-1-941501-32-0

Cover design by Rob Huberman
Book design by Rob Huberman
Illustrations by Joy Kolitsky

Printed in the United States of America

TABLE OF CONTENTS

About the Author 1

Author's Note 3

Preface 5

Chapter One
Opportunity 8

Chapter Two
Springtime in Vienna 10

Chapter Three
Dark Days at Home 11

Chapter Four
Brief Historical Background of Austria-Hungary 13

Chapter Five
Knowledge and Understanding 15

Chapter Six
Dark Days in Austria 16

Chapter Seven
Challenging Times 18

Chapter Eight
Knowing What Must Be Done 21

Chapter Nine
Taking Action 23

Chapter Ten
Shanghai: A Distant Refuge 25

Chapter Eleven
The Jews and Shanghai 28

Chapter Twelve
Jewish Life in the Ghetto 31

Chapter Thirteen
China After the War 32

Chapter Fourteen
Jewish Survivors and Their Stories of Rescue:
Most by the Efforts of Dr. Feng-Shan Ho 34

Chapter 15
Conclusion 37

Photos 38

Bibliography 64

About the Author

Robert Holden has been a lifelong educator, starting his teaching career in Ocean City at the Intermediate School in 1975, after graduating from Kutztown State College in Pennsylvania. He taught self-contained fourth grade for seven years and then started and taught the gifted/talented program (PACE Creative Program) for the balance of his career, retiring in 2006. In 1983, Holden received his Master's Degree in Elementary School Supervision from then Glassboro State College.

In approximately 1982 he created a well-received course about the Holocaust for his seventh grade G/T students. The course's success promped Holden to attend a Holocaust studies trip to Europe and Israel in 1997 (sponsored by the Richard Stockton College of New Jersey), where he had the opportunity to visit Holocaust sites such as Berlin's Wannsee Villa, Auschwitz-Birkenau in Poland and Theresienstadt in the Czech Republic. In Israel, he consulted with educators and museum personnel at Yad Vashem in Jerusalem.

In 2003 Holden served on the committee to revise the New Jersey State-mandated Holocaust education curriculum, and several years later he was awarded the "Honey and Maurice Axelrod Award" for his dedication to education about the Holocaust.

In 2006, (after retiring from Ocean City) Holden and 15 Canadian teachers, with BC and NJ ALPHA's sponsorship, made the 18-day pilgrimage to China to learn about Japanese aggression against the Chinese during WWII. Holden and the other teachers met survivors of Japanese aggression, which culminated with a secondary education curriculum guide about this chapter of history, and was co-written with Holden's longtime friend and colleague, Doug Cervi (currently Executive Director of the New Jersey Commission on Holocaust Education).

Titled, *The Nanking Massacre and Other Japanese Atrocities Committed During the Asia-Pacific War; 1931-1945*, the curriculum was published in 2007 and has been distributed to every school district in New Jersey, and is still available online at the NJCOHE's website. It was on this trip that Holden first visited the Shanghai Ghetto historic site, an inspiration for this book.

In 2007 he created and taught Holocaust and Genocide Studies at the Trocki Hebrew Academy in Egg Harbor Township, NJ, and supervised student teachers through Rowan University.

In 2009 Holden used a portion of his "Axelrod Award" earning to purchase books and materials for a new section of the Atlantic Cape Community College Cape May, NJ campus library's Holocaust Resource Center, It was designed and created by Holden, Library Director Grant Wilinski and ACCC CMC campus Librarian Leslie Murtha.

Holden's commitment to Holocaust and genocide education remains strong in retirement, and he has given numerous presentations about anti-Semitism, the rise of the Nazis, and the Holocaust. He is an original member of the Board of the South Jersey Holocaust Coalition, and is active in the Upper Township, NJ historical society and as its historian since 2018.

Holden's last book, *Upper Township and its Ten Villages*, was published by Arcadia Publishing Company in February of 2020.

He has been married to his beloved wife, Janice for more than 44 years. They have two children, Becky (husband Chris) and son, Ryan (fiancé Jen) and two granddaughters, Amelia, age 10, and Harper, age 8, who also love history like their pop-pop. Holden lives in Upper Township, Cape May County, NJ and enjoys kayaking, biking, and most of all, his restored 1947 Studebaker, Champion sedan.

Author's Note

Chinese people place the surname of individuals FIRST, so Feng Shan Ho would be Ho Feng Shan in Chinese. For a wider audience, his name will be written throughout this book as Feng-Shan Ho.

Virtually all photos in this book came at the courtesy of Eric Saul. I am indebted to him not only for his great knowledge of Dr. Ho, but also his advice and counsel as this book was edited.

Thanks to Rob Huberman at ComteQ Publishing who first gave me the encouragement to go forward with this story.

Thanks to Joy Kolitsky, the gifted illustrator for this book! Dear readers, Joy was once a fourth-grade student of mine at Ocean City Intermediate School (in about 1979-80) and even then I recognized her artistic talent! It was kismet that we were brought together again to complete this book after all these years. Joy has been just that; a joy to work with.

Thanks also to my wonderful and supportive wife, Janice who suffered from my many absences; even when I was home at the keyboard of my iMac. MY anchor always.

Thanks to dear friend, and fellow (now retired) Holocaust Educator Rich Flaim who was the "icing on the cake" as the final draft came back from him. His "imprimatur" made it all worthwhile.

Fittingly I saved the best for last – Thekla Lit and the BC ALPHA group who provided the financial support both for my 2006 trip to China to study *The Nanking Massacre* and after that for this book. It would not have happened without their encouragement and support.

The message for all readers is that we must accept and embrace *all* people of various religions and races if we are to succeed and become truly good human beings! The rash of anti-Asian attacks over the past two years in this country have been both shocking and horrifying.

It is my hope that this book will make our young people aware of the great humanity of men like Feng-Shan Ho, a good and decent Chinese man who saved people who were not of his race or creed.

He did this deed at risk to himself – but did it anyway for humanity!

He is to be forever revered.

Preface

There are oppressed people all over the world today who are continuously besieged and want freedom from their oppressors. We all need to be aware of violations of human rights around the world and speak up to everyone we meet to inform them if they aren't aware.

In today's world, Amnesty International has noted the ten worst situations of human rights violations. (You can easily read all about these terrible situations on line.) Amnesty notes: The horrible oppression of the Rohingya of Myanmar, the persecution of The Uyghurs of China, the oppressed Chinese people of Hong Kong, religious minorities in Egypt, asylum seekers in Hungary, oppression of the Palestinians in Israel, vicious attacks against civilians in Kenya, attacks against civilians and religious minorities in Pakistan, political prisoners in Russia, the torture and ill treatment of women and those critical of the government in Saudi Arabia, and war crimes and human rights violations in Syria.

These are just the tip of the iceberg of human rights violations worldwide.

People like you, dear reader, need to be aware of their plight and the lack of effort made to ensure the peace and freedom for people like these around the world.

Stories of rescue during the Holocaust are many, but the majority of these are not widely read. Most people, even those who study the Holocaust, could not begin to know each and every story of rescue which occurred during this horrific chapter of history!

Everyone who searches for these fantastic stories should keep in mind as they read, the great bravery and humanity of these people. Eli Wiesel once said, "These were not crusaders, but were determined to remain human." Making the choice to be an **upstander** and even go so far as to save another human being's life is not easy.

In her book, **The Courage to Care,** Dr. Carol Rittner, professor of Holocaust Studies at then Stockton College, wrote about several wonderful and brave people who desired to remain human and save Jews because it was the right thing to do. The book was later made into an award winning film.

Dr. Rittner profiles the rescued and also rescuers in her stories. Two of those rescued profiled in her book and film were Odette Myers, a young Jewish girl in Paris, and Emanuel Tanay, a young Jewish boy saved by Poles who placed him in a Catholic Monastery to hide.

The rescuers, special kind of people with amazing human skills, are portrayed as people who knew nothing else but to do the right thing and save oppressed people. This was as natural as breathing to them. They were supremely human in an inhumane world.

The rescuers profiled in her book were; Pastor and Magda Trocme' in the Village of Le Chambon-sur-Lignon, Marion P. Pritchard in Amsterdam who saved three Jewish children at great risk to herself, and Irene Opdyke, a Pole who worked as a cook and housekeeper for the Germans and saved an entire family of her Jewish friends right under the very nose (in the basement) of her Nazi Wehrmacht employer!

Google these names in order to read these and other stories of rescuers such as Nicholas Winton of England who while on a business trip to Austria and Czechoslovakia, saw the oppression of Jews there and became determined to do something about it. (He eventually saved hundreds of Jewish children via the now famous **Kindertransports** to Great Britain.)

Many of you may have read about Chiune Sugihara, the Japanese diplomat in Kaunas, Lithuania who decided to write visas for Jews to escape persecution. He worked endless hours to be sure everyone who needed a visa received it! And this was when the Japanese were allied with the Nazis!

The list of rescuers is seemingly endless and this should give us pause when we think that the world is purely evil and never contains any good. All of these rescuers became determined, each in their own way, to step up and do the right thing; to be *human* to their fellow man.

The subject of this book, Dr. Feng Shan Ho was focused, determined, and courageous in his rescue efforts in Vienna.

The lessons we learn from their (and his!) actions should serve us well. This story of Chinese diplomat, Feng-Shan Ho reveals one more rescuer who was determined to do the right thing and save Jews; this time, in Vienna and parts of Austria, from inevitable murder. He was always described as a man with a "compassionate heart".

He was a very humble man who did what he did, not for recognition or fame.

In 1999, this great man had a plaque and tree planted at Yad Vashem, Jerusalem on the *Avenue of the Righteous*. Here, you will read why.

Chapter One
Opportunity

Dr. Ho was sent to Vienna (from Istanbul, Turkey) in 1937 by the Nationalist Chinese government. His family was surely excited about this new adventure to Vienna, Austria.

From Istanbul, they took the famed Orient Express Train directly to Vienna. On the way they were able to sight-see in Sofia, Belgrade, and Budapest. Feng Shan Ho was on his way to his new promotion as First Secretary in the Chinese Legation.

A *legation* is a diplomatic group of people from a friendly country, led by a person who is not an ambassador, but has some decision-making power.

Leaving Istanbul in Turkey was not easy for him. Leaving your first posting must always be difficult; He had gotten used to the routine of being in Turkey and his family had all of the challenges of packing and planning, but the prospects ahead were great. After all, he spoke fluent German and he was looking forward to the new and different work that might be required.

The *Charge' d'Affaires* of the Legation, was Tong De-qian and he would meet with Feng-Shan Ho directly after their arrival to apprise him of his Duties as First Secretary.

Ho looked back on his life and career as he made this important move. He had come such a long way from the poverty of Yijang, where he grew up in Hunan Province.

In 1908 at the age of 7, he lost his father and now he wondered if he would be proud of his hardworking son. Feng Shan was named for the "Phoenix on the Mountain".

He had always been diligent and hardworking; values taught to him both at his Lutheran Mission School and later, at The College of Yale-in-China in the provincial capital of Changsha where he developed his lifelong dedication to: ***mens sana, corpore sana*** (sound mind, sound body).

He then attended the Ludwig Maximillian University in Munich where he mastered his German. In 1929, he received his doctorate (Magna Cum Laude) in political economics. It was a difficult journey, but he worked diligently and the hard work paid off. Throughout his life he was tireless in his pursuit of knowledge and self-improvement.

Ho possessed a dynamic, outgoing personality, boundless energy and a hot temper, offset by a quick wit and great sense of humor. A large part of him was very Chinese, and was firmly rooted in Confucian Principles. In fact, he named his two children after tenets of Confucianism, "Virtue" and "Decorum." A man of both intellect and passion, he strove all his life to balance the two. *"He knew he had been given many gifts from God, and felt they were not given to him solely for his own benefit but to do for others, for his fellow man."* said his pastor, Reverend Charles Kuo.

Back in 1935 he started his diplomatic career within the Foreign Ministry of the Republic of China with his first posting in Turkey. Living and working in Istanbul was challenging, but now he was here in Vienna two years later, and a new chapter of his life was playing out. He was genuinely excited about the new assignment!

Chapter Two
Springtime in Vienna

The spring of 1937 bloomed early in Vienna. The city, to which Ho and his family arrived was in the very center of Europe and was known for its music and good food. Exiting the train and arriving in so lovely a city was exhilarating for Ho and his family! The city was truly beautiful in a much different way than was Istanbul.

There was the Wiener Staatsoper (State Opera) building, which was not only a historic landmark, but the local transportation junction as well.

Behind the Opera House there was the famed Eck Café of the Hotel Sacher in Philharmonikergasse. Then there was the shopping promenade, the Kartnerstrasse, where shop fronts were covered with beautiful facades. The most famous landmark was the Stephansdom (St. Stephen's Cathedral). Mozart was married there, as well as countless Hapsburg Emperors.

In addition, there was the Schottentor on the Ringstrasse, the old grand gate into the city.

Dr. Ho wrote in his autobiography **My Forty Years as a Diplomat**, about his initial contacts and reactions after arriving in Vienna:

"*Not long after I arrived, people were asking me to speak. I spoke to numerous groups and also went to numerous coffeehouses around the city to talk about Chinese culture. One spoke only English at this club. There were clubs of other nationalities, including many German Clubs. I spoke at many of these clubs, too.*

The audiences were very enthusiastic. I made many friends.

I was kept very busy doing this. The audiences were eager to learn, but by and large they were woefully ignorant of China.

The important fact was that the common man in Austria supported Chinese resistance against Japan."

Chapter Three
Dark Days at Home

In 1931, Dr. Ho knew that Japan had invaded Manchuria and both occupied and terrorized its citizens. Japan planned the invasion and occupation of Manchuria as its economic "lifeline"; robbing it of its natural resources and agricultural goods. The Japanese public approved, because they were convinced this would save their economy after the Great Depression. There seemed to be no anti-war sentiment in Japan. The Western media, however reported events such as atrocities and civilian bombing with chemical and biological weaponry, and it aroused considerable antipathy towards Japan.

Thousands of Chinese citizens were murdered and the world did little or nothing to stop it. *The League of Nations* attempted to intervene and offered to set up a "neutral zone" between China proper and Manchuria, but this did not last.

The United States would eventually decide to cut off oil and scrap metal exports to Japan, but it was really too late and ineffective; only stirring opposition to US efforts (seen by Japan as interference) toward peace in the Pacific. Tensions between the Empire of Japan and the Republic of China were heightened. The Japanese Army moved quickly to conquer and consolidate their power. The Army had taken full control. Tokyo sent more troops and eventually formed a puppet state in Manchuria, now called *Manchukuo*, with the deposed Qing Dynasty Emperor as its head.

The Kuomintang (Nationalist) government of China refused to recognize the state of Manchukuo, but formed a truce in 1933. Thereafter there were numerous incidents at the border. The Japanese were gradually getting a sense of how easy it might be to invade China, and take the country completely. By 1932, Japan had expanded its forces in Manchuria to about 60,500 men, and it was growing - for the coming invasion of China.

In 1937, the Japanese invaded China in a staged provocation at the Marco Polo Bridge in a village outside of Beijing called Wanping. This incident would set off the actual beginning of World War Two, when Japanese forces insisted on coming into the town and the Chinese, in their defense, opened fire. A ceasefire was later negotiated but the Japanese were determined to make inroads further into China.

By July of 1937, they had 180 thousand troops inside China, and an escalated war was assured.

Ho spoke in his autobiography about this Japanese aggression in China while in Vienna:

"The secretary of an organization asked me to talk about Sino-Japanese relations. I spent two weeks collecting evidence of Japanese aggression in China.

"The most important evidence, I concluded was the content of a secret memorandum from the Japanese premier on July 15, 1927 to Emperor Hirohito about conquering the world. About two thousand people attended. The talk was a great success. Commercial publishers sought to enlarge my lectures and expand them into a book. A 103-page booklet in German was published called **China Defends Herself***.*

"I also took the opportunity to form the **Chinese-Austrian Cultural Association** *with a membership of about two hundred. They came from all levels of society."*

Chapter Four
Brief Historical Background of Austria-Hungary

Dr. Ho, of course, did his research and studied the history of the country to which he was to be newly assigned. Politically, Vienna, as the capital of the united nation of Austria-Hungary had once been ruled by the Habsburg dynasty for 640 years.

The first emperor of the two conjoined nations, Austria and Hungary, Franz Josef, had come to power in 1848 after the revolutions that had ransacked so many countries and toppled their governments. There was once an Austria and a Hungary as two separate nations, but since the Austrian (Germans) were dominant, Hungary and the Magyars, were brought into its sphere of influence and domination.

The year 1848 was one that saw the poor and oppressed of Europe rise up and revolt in nearly every European country. Germany, Poland, Italy, France, Austria, and Hungary, saw its people revolt and take on a new form of Nationalism. Many escaped this debacle and came to America; "The Land of Opportunity". The first great wave of German, Poles, Italian, Slavic, Russian, and Irish immigration to America began in the critical year of 1848. (The Irish came predominantly to escape the **Potato Famine** which killed a million citizens from 1845-1849.)

The years from 1848-1914 saw a surge across Europe in Nationalistic pride and love of country. People in each country took pride in their language and national culture. Children for the first time were educated in national schools which encouraged learning and speaking the nation's single language, love of country, and national unity. For the first time, many experienced flying their nation's flag.

When the First World War started in 1914, Austria was on the side of Germany and the Central Powers. It was Great Britain, France and Russia as the Allies pitted against Germany, Austria-Hungary, and Italy. Italy switched to the Allies side in 1915.

The beloved old Emperor Franz Josef (nicknamed, *The Old Man*), who had ruled his country with an iron fist for nearly 70 years, died in 1916 before the end of the war and his heir, Charles took over the throne until he abdicated in 1918, ruling a greatly diminished Austria now separated from its sister country, Hungary.

The Austro-Hungarian Empire had collapsed after World War One.

The war had not gone well for Austria-Hungary and the country did not realize any gains from the Treaty of Versailles in 1919. In fact, the country was split back into its former components; Austria and Hungary, with some territory given to its neighbors. Such was the result of being part of the Central powers and allied with Germany, The Ottoman Empire, and initially, Italy.

Chapter Five
Knowledge and Understanding

Dr. Ho also knew: Austria had been a republic since 1919, but was now under threat from Germany as he prepared to enter the country.

He knew that the Nazi Party in Germany was growing in power through the late 20's and into the 1930's and exerted its influence in Austria, encouraging Austrian Nationalists, and eventually National Socialists, who wanted Austria to merge with Germany.

In May, 1932, the Christian-Socialist Party formed a government with Engelbert Dollfuss as Chancellor (Prime Minister).

Dollfuss took steps to curtail anti-Semitism by outlawing discrimination against the Jews in housing and jobs. By this time, in 1933, Hitler had maneuvered to become the Chancellor of Germany. Actually, he was given the job by the aged President, Paul von Hindenburg, who thought that he and his ministers would keep the peace and could "control" Hitler and the Nazi Party. Hitler was strongly in favor of the annexation of his homeland, Austria.

Dollfuss sought help from his Southern neighbor, Italy, ruled since 1922 by the fascist dictator, Benito Mussolini. Dollfuss hoped that Mussolini would not appreciate a Nazi government on its northern border. Mussolini was indeed suspicious of Hitler's intentions.

Chapter Six
Dark Days in Austria

Dollfuss outlawed the Austrian Nazi Party, however it continued to operate illegally.

On July 25, 1934, Austrian Nazis occupied the Parliament building and murdered Dollfuss.

Ho, at the time, considered this an outrageous and unwise move. Their leaders were arrested and executed, but the *handwriting was on the wall*. Ho fully realized that Germany was determined to take over Austria.

This was eventually bound to make Dr. Ho's job more difficult because of his feelings for the country and the fact that his friends were now in great danger; Jews especially; as they had the most to fear from any takeover by the Nazis, because they were targeted for eradication by Nazi policies.

Ho had hopes that the new Chancellor, Kurt Schuschnigg, who had received guarantees of sovereignty from Britain, France, and Italy in April, 1935 would be successful in his resistance.

Mussolini, however, was overwhelmed by worshipful visits from Hitler and decided to change course. In 1936 Italy formed the Axis alliance with Germany. Italy no longer supported Austria.

Ho had read in the International Press that Schuschnigg wanted to meet with Hitler directly and voice his opposition to German (Nazi) influence in Austria.

The two men met, but Hitler was an overwhelming force. He insisted that the Austrian Interior ministry be led by a Nazi. Schuschnigg resisted Hitler's screaming threats. One meeting was an hours long diatribe by Hitler and, in fact, Schuschnigg threatened Hitler that he would hold a national *plebiscite* on March 13th.

A *plebiscite* is actually a direct vote of the electorate/members of the country, in this case asking the Austrians if they wanted to join Germany as one nation or not.

Hitler had other ideas and stated that if the plebiscite were held, he would invade the country immediately. He screamed at Schuschnigg that he had troops waiting at the border and would use them if he had to. Schuschnigg continued to resist. The Nazis invaded, and occupied the country the day before the scheduled plebiscite on March 12th.

Two days later, Hitler triumphantly paraded through Vienna. and was welcomed by most Austrians with open arms. Why? Most Austrians spoke German and Hitler after all, was born in Austria. In addition, the Nazis had already infiltrated many Austrian nationalist organizations and government positions and had laid the groundwork for this annexation, (called in German, *Der Anschluss*) The propaganda campaign in Austria in the lead up to the Anschluss was enormous.

At the time of this Anschluss in March, 1938, over 185,000 Jews lived in Austria, with 170,00 residing in Vienna. The persecution of the Jews was now more virulent than what had happened to them in Germany.

Chapter Seven
Challenging Times

Dr. Ho found through diplomatic channels, that Hitler had declared that Germany and Austria were now one nation. Austria was fully annexed and Austria now was to be known as *Ostmark*, the bulwark of the East against communism. Artur Seyss-Inquart, was named as Interior Minister and eventual governor-general of the occupied country.

The offices of Vienna's Jewish community and Zionists Institutions were closed. Jewish bankers and businessmen were arrested and sent to Dachau. Jews were banned from any public activities.

In May, the Nuremberg Laws which had been passed in Germany in 1935 now were in effect in Austria, and these laws forcibly separated Jews from Austrian society and deprived them of their livelihoods, and even their citizenship!

After the Nazi takeover, on March 12, 1938, all foreign embassies and legations were closed. Ho got orders to dissolve the legation and set up a Consulate-General. He now had to report to the Chinese Embassy in Berlin, the capital of the conjoined German-speaking nations. Ho was horrified by the fanatical welcome of Hitler and the Nazis.

As Consul-General, Ho was invited to meet Hitler, whom he described: *"He was a short little man. He had a ridiculous moustache. He was an unspeakable martinet."* Dr. Ho was always a good judge of character!

The Chinese embassy was no doubt demoted because of Japanese influences; since Germany and Japan had formed an Axis pact of support for one another. This would be an advantage for the Germans because now the Austrian government spoke and acted as

One German Nation; Germany and Austria combined. Ho worried that his family had arrived in a country soon to be ruled by the Nazis.

Dr. Ho was given orders to set up the offices and be The Chinese Consulate General. It was located at 3 Beethoven Platz. The street was named for the great German composer, Beethoven, who lived for most of his life in Vienna.

He received his appointment in May, 21, 1938. Now, the legation staff was simply Dr. Ho and his one subordinate, a Vice-Consul. The family stayed in a hotel in the Stadt Park (city park) nearby his Legation on Beethoven Platz, a large three-story building with an elevator.

Ho spoke fluent English and German and had many friends in the city; a substantial number of whom were Jewish.

He was provided an office in the hotel on the second floor next to a large guest room.

Ho recalled,

"At this time, the anti-Jewish campaign intensified. Many Jewish-owned shops were ransacked by Nazis and their owners deported to concentration camps."

Ho himself, along with other customers had once been held at gunpoint by a roving band of Nazis who stormed into Vienna's cafes looking for Jews. He was outraged by what he had witnessed.

Feng Shan Ho was clearly a man with a conscience. The Jews of Austria were increasingly in danger, and they needed help. Ho knew that someone had to take responsibility!

But it was his own country of China that Ho was most concerned about at this time.

China was being intimidated by Japan after its invasion of Manchuria back in 1931. By July 7th of 1937, the conflicts, which had started in Beijing, culminated into open warfare, with the Japanese Army brutally attacking the capital, Nanking, on December 13, 1937, massacring as many as 300 thousand innocents into January of 1938.

The Chinese people, long seen as subhuman by the Japanese fought against overwhelming military odds, but were quickly overwhelmed and brutalized.

Ho's mind was certainly on his homeland as he accepted this new posting in Vienna.

By November of 1938 and the **pogrom** called **Kristallnacht**, (a **pogrom** is an organized massacre or wave of violence against a particular ethnic group; in this case the Jews) things were bad for the Jews, but circumstances had also gotten much worse for the Chinese, with Japanese military aggression against China.

The horrific event of **Kristallnacht**, also known as **The Night of Broken Glass**, was where Nazis rose up across Germany and Austria on the night between November 9th and 10th, and destroyed Jewish businesses, burned down a thousand synagogues and arrested thousands of innocent people throwing them into concentration camps. It was clearly a violent and often deadly riot against the Jewish people. The situation for Jews throughout Germany and Austria became rapidly much more difficult and terrifying. Austria had over 185 thousand Jews, most of whom lived in Vienna.

Less than a month after the Anschluss, many Austrian Jews were evicted from their homes and by 1938 many were deported to Dachau and Buchenwald concentration camps. Most were released after signing an agreement that they would leave the country.

All adults were forced to take the middle name of Sara (females) and Israel (males) and had their passports stamped with a large red "J". Along with this rule, Jews were banned from all public places. By September, the Jewish community organization, **The Gemeinde** was feeding over half of the remaining Jews in Vienna.

It quickly became apparent that the only way for Jews to escape Nazism and certain death was to leave Europe.

Chapter Eight
Knowing What Must be Done

Lines formed at emigration offices at dawn even though they didn't open until noon.

The adults had to sign paperwork, pay fees and then turn over their entire remaining money to the Nazis before they would receive their temporary passports.

There were visits to consular offices to obtain exit visas, transit visas, or applications for the very limited number of entry visas to the United States. This limited number was due to their **quota** system.

(A **quota** is a system of limiting, by nationality or religion, the number of immigrants who may enter a country; in this case, the U.S., which had established these quotas by legislation in 1921.) The U.S. had this very restrictive quota system and there were definitely members of the State Department who were anti-Semitic at this time; unwilling to make allowances for the plight of any Jews, let alone Austrian Jews, to escape to freedom.

Ten thousand people left Vienna in the first month that the emigration center was open.

Many were forced at the last moment to change their destination and go wherever they could with available visas.

In order to leave Austria, they had to provide proof of emigration, usually a visa from a foreign nation, or a valid boat ticket. This was difficult because of the *Evian Conference,* where 31 out of 32 countries refused to accept Jewish immigrants. This Conference, (held in Evian, France) which met in July of 1938, saw delegates from 32 countries meet to discuss the quotas for Jews which would be allowed to enter the countries of the conference participants. The meeting lasted nine days but even after all these discussions, the

United States and even Great Britain offered excuses for not letting in more refugees!

The conference was actually a propaganda coup for the Nazis who crowed that it was astounded that foreign countries criticized their treatment of the Jews, but none of them wanted to open their doors to them! President Franklin Roosevelt had not even sent a high-level diplomat to Evian, and so the U.S. remained unwilling to ease their immigration restrictions.

The only country willing to accept refugee Jews was the Dominican Republic which offered to accept 100 thousand refugees.

Chapter Nine
Taking Action

Dr. Ho was one of the first few international diplomats to take action to save Jews and issued visas to any Jew who requested one. There were, indeed, others who provided visas to Jews. Men like Frank Foley in the British Embassy in Berlin, and Pio Perucchi with Candido Porta who were Swiss Consular Officers in Milan, who issued thousands of illegal visas to Jews against the policies of the Swiss government in 1938-1939.

In late 1938, Dr. Ho acting against the orders of his superior, Chen Jie, the Chinese Ambassador in Berlin started to issue exit visas to desperate Jews destined for Shanghai for humanitarian reasons. Chen Jie in Berlin, however, wanted to maintain good diplomatic relations with Germany and did not want to oppose Hitler's antisemitic policies. Acting against the orders of his superiors, coupled with possible recriminations of the Austrian Nazis, made Ho's work extremely risky.

In fact, Ambassador Chen Jie called Ho on the phone and ordered him to desist the visas.

Ho, of course, refused, deciding to follow the initial "liberal" policy of writing as many visas possible, regardless of what the ambassador said.

Less than a year after the Chinese Consulate was established, the Nazis confiscated the Jewish-owned building which housed the Consul's offices. Consul-General Ho asked the Chinese government for funds to relocate the Consulate. The Chinese government refused, saying that China was at war with Japan and had no funds available.

Ho found smaller facilities for the consulate at 22 Johannes Gasse. He moved there and paid all the expenses out of his own pocket!

By the end of July, 1938, The Chinese Consulate had issued more than 1,200 Visas to Shanghai.

Dr. Ho was modest in the descriptions of his efforts but was determined to save as many Jews as possible. He went to great lengths to save people, even secretly communicating with religious and charitable organizations to save as many Jews as they could.

Sadly, the Viennese Jewish Community was officially dissolved in November, 1942. By the end of the war, more than 65,000 Austrian Jews had died in Nazi concentration camps and ghettos.

Dr. Ho had left Vienna by then in 1940. There was little more he could do. As the Nazis swept across Europe conquering countries in its path, their policy had switched from coerced emigration to murder.

In all, 128,500; nearly 70 percent of Austria's 185,246 Jews had emigrated. Thousands escaped due to the efforts of Consul-General Ho!

Chapter Ten
Shanghai: A Distant Refuge

The port city of Shanghai was for many Jews, after the terrible events of Kristallnacht, the last refuge that could be reached without a passport, visa, or affidavit, unlike the US or Canada, and all that was needed to make the trip was money for a ticket.

Between June and August 1939 alone, approximately 14,000 German-speaking refugees reached Shanghai, and many more were to follow.

Ho was more than likely the first diplomat to take this action to save the Jews to Shanghai.

He practiced a liberal visa policy, authorizing the issuing of exit visas to any or all who asked. Having been turned down by other consulates, the Jews soon discovered they could get visas at the Chinese Consulate.

How did these visas work? Just what is a *visa*?

A *visa* is an endorsement on a passport indicating that the holder of that passport is allowed to enter, leave, or stay for a specified period of time in the country.

Ho's idea was ingenious. The documents were simply to be *Exit visas*; a visa as a means of escape. This visa, as proof of a destination, was necessary for Jews to be allowed to leave Austria and escape to Shanghai. Shanghai was an open port city without immigration controls and occupied by the Japanese Army. Anyone could enter without a visa.

The visas issued by Ho had only one destination – Shanghai, and these *Shanghai visas* would provide Jewish refugees in Austria with the proof of emigration required by the Nazis to leave.

Twelve hundred visas were issued by Ho in his first three months of holding office as the Consul-General. Eventually, the trickle would turn into a flood and thousands of visas were written; at great risk to Dr. Ho whose signature was on each visa. No one knew just how erratic and irrational these Austrian Nazis could be, and at any time, they could have shut him down or worse. These visas, although not necessary to enter Shanghai, allowed the Jews to leave Vienna to safety.

It is significant that these exit visas allowed escapees to use the documents to obtain a transit visa and escape elsewhere upon arrival. Dr. Ho's signed visas were the golden tickets to freedom and survival. Many of the Jews stayed for a short time in Shanghai, but many later left for the U.S., Australia, Canada, or the Philippines.

Jews across Austria heard about the *Shanghai visas* and they were desperate to escape, so the name *Shanghai* spread like wildfire.

The risks continued, although the Austrian Nazis didn't seem to want to risk an international incident by insulting the Chinese.

Until Italy entered the war in June, 1940 (Mussolini only risked entry into the war when he could ride on Germany's' coat tails/military victories) most Jewish refugees left from Italy on the Lloyd-Tristino Line. The Jews bankrupted themselves to buy first class tickets. One ship brought 3,600 refugees to Shanghai on seven voyages made between December 1938 and February, 1939. Because the Nazis had confiscated nearly everything the Jews owned, they were permitted to take only a few personal possessions (but no money or valuables) and most stepped off the boats well-dressed but penniless.

Later groups were forced to make the trip by land through Manchuria or Vladivostok.

Ho continued to issue these visas until he was ordered to return to China in May, 1940.

This was likely because the issuing of these visas was irritating the Austrians who were certainly under pressure from the Nazis in Berlin. The Chinese may have been worrying about Ho's safety.

In his memoir, Ho would later write:

"Since the Anschluss, the persecution of the Jews by Hitler's Devils became increasingly fierce. I spared no effort in using any means possible to help, thus saving countless Jews."

It should be noted that in his memoir, Dr. Ho never mentions the great risks he surely took to save so many people. He never boasts nor brags of his great accomplishments, but simply describes what he had to do. In fact, after all these years, historians have had to carefully search for details of Ho's bravery in his efforts to save the Jews of Vienna.

Most of these Jews were strangers to him, but some of these people were his friends. Dr. Ho knew the visas were not exactly "Shanghai Visas"; most people who escaped would not be remaining in Shanghai.

"I knew that the Chinese Visas to Shanghai were 'in name' only. In reality, it was a means for them to find a way to get to the U.S., England or other destinations," he recalled.

The exact number of visas he signed is unknown, but he signed his 200th visa in June, 1938 and the 1,906th visa was signed on October 27th, 1938. The number of Jews he saved must certainly be in the thousands, perhaps in the tens of thousands. In his biography there was no "Schindler's List" of names. After the war, the survivors were scattered all over the world. Most of the adults who lined up in front of the Chinese Consulate to obtain the special visas were gone, and they did not necessarily tell their children the details of how the family escaped.

Chapter Eleven
The Jews and Shanghai

Built by Russian Jews in 1927 in the Hongkew District in Northern Shanghai, the Ohel Moshe Synagogue was the primary religious destination for Jewish refugees who flooded into the city. In this "Miracle of Shanghai", noted by Holocaust scholar David Kranzler, about 20,000 refugees settled around the synagogue in an area called *The Restricted Sector for Stateless Refugees* but more commonly known as *The Jewish Ghetto*. Life was harsh, with as many as 30 sharing a room.

Betty (Ilse Kohn) Grebenschikoff came to Shanghai at the age of 8. In her memoir, ***Once My Name Was Sara***, she describes life there from 1937 through 1950, as a German refugee from Berlin. She arrived with her sister and parents. Betty remembered: "*The internment of stateless refugees began in Shanghai, a little over a year after the Japanese bombed Pearl Harbor on December 7, 1941. The Japanese Military Command decreed (in 1937) that the refugees were to move into a designated area in Hongkew, measuring about one mile by two and a half miles. Those arriving after the year 1937 were not affected by this order.*"

Life was very difficult for the refugees who lived here. The climate was hot and humid in the summer and the winters were cold, bitter, and harsh.

Life in the ghetto was easier for children but much more difficult for parents who faced the daily stress of getting necessary food, securing needed medical supplies and medicines, preparing for blackouts during American bombing raids, and all of the frictions which normally develop in families who are forced to remain in space restricted areas.

Japanese soldiers excluded all people from the designated area from the parks and recreational areas. The Chinese had many shops but the refugees opened many different stores themselves, some no bigger than a closet.

For those who couldn't afford new things, some Shanghai citizens sold second hand items on the street. Just about anything could be gotten from these street sellers; including a wide variety of diseases.

Disease and malnutrition was widespread in the ghetto. There was a hospital in the designated area, but it was woefully understaffed and underequipped. With the cold being so intense in the winter, many died from the cold. Medicines were nearly impossible to procure to treat the sick.

Mr. Ghoya, the Japanese Commander required special passes to leave the designated area. All people needed passes to get out for work, school, or other duties.

The Japanese soldiers were tough but not cruel; at least not to the people from the designated area. They were merciless to the Chinese.

According to the Japanese census, 15,000 stateless people were housed in the ghetto. Of these, 99.95 % were Jews which included nearly all of those who had fled the German occupied areas in Europe since 1937. All of these Jews were considered "stateless," without a country of origin.

After the war was over in 1945, the Japanese soldiers all but disappeared and liberation came for the many allied enemy nationals who had been imprisoned in detention camps.

The city was jubilant with the influx of released prisoners and new American soldiers arriving in Shanghai.

The barriers were gone and the Chinese Nationalists (led by Chiang Kai-Shek) were back in power. American soldiers, sailors, and marines flocked into China as the Americans made their headquarters there and took control of the port of Shanghai.

Most of the European Jews had left for other destinations, but they always looked upon Shanghai as their second home calling it their "Noah's Ark".

Note: There is a Shanghai Jewish Refugees Museum located there in Shanghai today which can be visited daily at specified times for 50 RMB ($7 U.S.)

Chapter Twelve
Jewish Life in the Ghetto

Much of the ghetto in Shanghai is gone, but the author visited the ghetto and synagogue in August of 2006. The Ohel Moshe Synagogue and some houses still remain that were built by Russian Jews in 1927, and these are reminders that this city saved tens of thousands of Jews fleeing Vienna and Austria from 1938-1940.

Twenty thousand refugees settled in and around the synagogue in an area just 2.68 square miles called, *The Restricted Sector for Stateless Refugees*, or simply, *The Jewish Ghetto*. As a closed area, entry and exit passes had to be obtained to work outside of Hongkew. Anyone needing to leave had to be approved by the Japanese authorities. People approved to leave had to wear a round metal pin on their coats or jackets.

The Japanese controlled the city, home to more than 100 thousand Shanghai residents. The Chinese, despite certain threats by the Japanese welcomed their new residents with great compassion.

The area around the museum is called the Tilanqiao Historic District, which contains well preserved living quarters used by the refugees. As many as thirty shared a room in this ghetto but at least everyone was alive and well.

"Little Vienna" is an intersection of two roads: Zhoushan Road and Huoshan Road and this once had European style cafes and shops. Tours are available by appointment. (The author easily arrived at the historic area via a Shanghai taxi.)

Chapter Thirteen
China After the War

Dr. Ho spent the remaining years of the Second World War involved in China's struggle against Japan. The war's end brought more complications for him.

Japan had waged a war of horrible aggression against the Chinese and it is estimated that as many as 34 million were killed during this intense Japanese War of Aggression against China through 1945.

In 1947, Dr. Ho began a nine-year tenure as ambassador to Egypt, and seven other Middle Eastern countries.

But even China was embroiled all this time in a Civil War. The Nationalists led by Chaing Kai-Sheck were fighting for control of the country against Mao Zedong and his Communists.

The Communists overcame the Nationalists and after the Communist victory in 1949, Ho followed the Nationalist government in Taiwan. He later served as the ambassador from Taiwan (The Republic of China) to other countries such as Mexico, Bolivia, and Columbia.

Ho retired in 1973 and settled in San Francisco where he began to write his memoir, *My Forty Years as a Diplomat.* It is a modest and straightforward autobiography, reprinted in 2010 by his son, Monto, a Chinese-American Microbiologist and Infectious disease doctor, and his daughter, Manli Ho, who was a reporter for the Boston Globe.

Feng-Shan Ho died in 1997 at the age of 96, attended by his wife and daughter. Until his death, he had lived a modest existence, devoting himself to writing, to his church, and to his community. He was a founding member of the Lutheran Church in San Francisco and a trustee of the Yale-China Association. His memoir was first published in 1990.

In the year 2000, Israel posthumously bestowed upon Ho the title, **Righteous Among the Nations**, one of its highest civil honors for his work in saving Austrian Jews in a ceremony at Yad-Vashem, Jerusalem attended by the Chinese Ambassador to Israel and many Israeli dignitaries.

A medal and certificate of honor were given to his two children Monto and Manli Ho, and his name was added to *The Honor Wall* in the *Garden of the Righteous*.

When asked why he decided to save the Jews of Vienna, he responded simply:

"I thought it only natural to feel compassion and want to help. From the standpoint of humanity, that is the way it should be."

Dr. Feng Shan Ho is one of only two Chinese to be considered for the honor of *Righteous Among the Nations*. The other was Pan Yun-shun, who received the title in 1995 after sheltering a Jewish girl during the occupation of part of the Soviet Union.

Dr. Ho has also received numerous posthumous awards of recognition from a variety of countries.

The U.S. Senate passed a resolution in 2008 honoring Ho's deeds. A commemorative plaque was placed on the former Chinese Consulate building in Vienna which is now the Ritz Carlton Hotel.

Dr. Feng Shan Ho's courage and humility in carrying out his work is an example to be read about and emulated by young people everywhere.

"He Who Saves One Life, Saves the World Entire"-
Mishnah Sanhedrin 4:5

Chapter Fourteen

Jewish Survivors and Their Stories of Rescue; Most by the Efforts of Dr. Feng-Shan Ho

The efforts of Feng-Shan Ho saved Jews who might otherwise have perished, and thus their families grew after the war.

Here are just a few stories of survival; most made possible by the courageous and selfless efforts of Dr. Feng-Shan Ho, who continued to write exit visas for Austrian Jews through 1940.

Betty Grebenschikoff - (A Berlin, Germany Jewish refugee.) After a long time spent in the ghetto, Betty and her husband Oleg were determined to leave Shanghai by 1950. They took a train to Tientsin then a ship to Hong Kong. From there, they were unable to board a ship to Australia due to Betty's advanced pregnancy. Thanks to Sir Horace Kadoorie (He was an industrialist and philanthropist who set up the school that became a haven for Jewish refugee children in Shanghai and whose family were originally Iraqi Jews), they were flown out to Sydney, Australia in 1950 after much difficulty with paper work. Her daughter, Jennifer was born there a few weeks later. They would live there for many years afterward before eventually coming to the United States in 1953.

Hans Kraus – He tried desperately to pass through a long line of people waiting at the Chinese Consulate. As he looked around, he saw the Chinese Consul's car about to enter the Consulate. The car's window was open and he thrust his visa application paper through the window. Later he got as telephone call to come and pick up his visa! Hans and four family members left Vienna for Shanghai.

Hugo Seeman – His family owned a department store in Austria before the Nazi takeover. They obtained visas from the Chinese Consulate (Dr. Ho's work) on October 12, 1938 and left on the Trans-Siberian railway which took them to Shanghai by way of the Soviet Union.

Eric Goldstaub – He was a 17 year old Viennese Jew, who had been turned down by 50 other consulates in Vienna before he went to the Chinese Consulate and met with Dr. Ho. In his testimony to Yad Vashem, Eric wrote: *"I spent days, weeks, and months visiting one foreign consulate after another trying to obtain a visa for me, my parents and our near relatives numbering some 20 people."* Finally, on July 20, 1938, he received 20 Chinese visas from Dr. Ho for all of his people. But then, during *Kristallnacht*, Eric and his father were arrested and sent to concentration camps. Eric continues, *"The fact that we had a visa for China as well as ship tickets for the end of December (via Genoa, Italy) enabled us to be released within a few days and we were on our way by train to Italy and liberty to China."*

Karl Lang – During the infamous *Kristallnacht* pogrom, he was one of the Austrian Jews hauled before the Gestapo to Dachau (the very first in Germany) concentration camp. His frantic wife, Katerina made the rounds of the consulates. In the words of their daughter Marian: *"Word got out that the Chinese consulate was issuing visas. Mother got a visa for my father with an end destination visa to Shanghai. I took our passports to the Gestapo headquarters to get them stamped. My father was in Dachau from November 1938 until February, 1939. He was released and had to sign a paper that said he would leave Austria within 48 hours."*

Her father left the country in time, and was able to go to England, where he was later joined by his family.

Bernard Grossfeld – Bernard and his parents in Vienna were also granted visas by Feng Shan Ho for travel to Shanghai thanks to which his father, Morris was released from Dachau concentration camp. In July, 1939, Bernard's family took a train from Vienna to Genoa, where they boarded a ship on a two-month voyage to Shanghai.

Fritz Heiduschka – After his arrest in mid-June, 1938, his wife Margarete obtained a visa from Dr. Ho, for travel to Shanghai. At first, both headed for Trieste, Italy, then together with their daughter, Hedy, they boarded an Italian ship bound for Shanghai.

When the boat stopped at Colombo, Ceylon, Margarete changed her mind and decided to continue to the Philippines, where they remained through the Japanese occupation, and until the end of the war.

Lilith-Sylvia Doron – Currently living in Israel, she related that she met Dr. Ho accidentally as both watched Hitler's entry into Vienna on March of 1938, which was accompanied with physical assaults on the city's Jews. In her words, *"Ho, who knew my family, accompanied me home. He stated that thanks to his diplomatic status, they would not dare harm us as long as he remained in our home. He continued to visit our home on a permanent basis to protect us from the Nazis."* When Lilith's brother Karl was arrested and taken to Dachau camp, he was released thanks to a visa by the Chinese Consulate. Lilith and her brother left for Palestine in November, 1939, on the strength of the Chinese visa that was of course meant for another destination - Shanghai.

Leya Vardi – Her family used the Shanghai visa to leave and head North to Sweden.

The Rosenberg Family – Kristallnacht in Austria began on the morning of Nov. 10th. That day, Consul General Feng-Shan Ho had an encounter with the Gestapo (secret Police), who appeared at the home of his Jewish friends, the Rosenbergs. They came in to arrest the residents and "search" the house. Dr. Ho had provided the Rosenbergs with visas to Shanghai and had come to their home that morning to escort them to the train station. Although the Gestapo agents pulled a gun on him, Ho was able to thwart them so that his friends could leave safely.

It should be pointed out dear readers, that none of these stories of rescue were ever related by Dr. Ho. himself. He was too modest for that! These stories came to light later after the Jews' survival.

Chapter Fifteen
Conclusion

The story of Dr. Feng-Shan Ho's bravery in the face of despicable barbarity is to be admired and that bravery should be emulated as much as possible by those who read his story.

This means you, dear reader! Stand up always for the oppressed and downtrodden and be strong in the face of racism, prejudice, and hatred of others. Always be humane in your treatment of others different than you!

All of those who rescued Jews and other Nazi-oppressed people stepped up and demonstrated their selflessness and humanity.

As French resident of Le Chambon-sur-Lignon and rescuer of French Jews, Magda Trocme once said, *"Are you thinking that we are all brothers, or not? Then let us try to help. There will come a time when you will need a kind of courage, a decision of your own. Not about other people, but about yourself. I would say nothing more."*

Dear reader, if you do believe we are all brothers in this world, you would do nothing else but help someone in need. Again, remember the quote noted above from the Talmud:

"He Who Saves One Life Saves the World Entire"- Mishnah Sanhedrin 4:5

This is the very definition of being human in a world where decent human beings are challenged every day to do the right thing, when facing moral dilemmas.

We must try to display this special kind of courage in our everyday lives; speaking out against injustice, stopping bullying, aiding when others are in danger, and rescuing those in need.

Remember these words by Feng-Shan Ho:

"I thought it only natural to feel compassion and want to help. From the standpoint of humanity, that is the way it should be."

Dr. Feng Shan Ho as a new diplomat for China, 1937.
(Photo courtesy of Dr. Ho's family)

Dr. Ho's diplomatic passport with his signature in English at the bottom.
(Photo courtesy of Dr. Ho's family)

Feng Shan Ho, his wife, and first-born child (son), Monto arrive in Vienna after the long train ride from Istanbul, 1937 (Joy Kolitsky)

Vienna in Spring (Joy Kolitsky)

The Stephansdom (Main Cathedral)
(Joy Kolitsky)

The Vienna Staatsoper (State Opera
House) (Joy Kolitsky)

Dr. Ho speaks to many varied groups of people throughout the city of Vienna.
(Joy Kolitsky)

Dissolution of Austria-Hungary after World War I (id.wilipedia.org)

Nazi Anschluss, March, 1938 (UShmm.org)

Nazi Anschluss propaganda posters like this one were displayed in Austria, circa 1938: "One People, One Nation, One Leader"
This poster was designed to influence skeptical Austrians.

Chancellor Engelbert Dollfuss; murdered by the Nazis in 1934. (Joy Kolitsky)

Chancellor Kurt Schuschnigg, Dollfuss's successor and leader of the Austrian Fatherland Party, who confronted Hitler in a meeting before the Anschluss. (Joy Kolitsky)

Hitler enters Vienna triumphantly in his massive Mercedes limousine after Anschluss (takeover) of Austria, March, 1938. (Photo courtesy of Eric Saul)

Jewish boy forced to paint the word Jude (Jew) on the outer wall of his apartment building. (Photo courtesy of Eric Saul)

Older Jews forced to scrub streets of Vienna on their hands and knees. (Photo courtesy of Eric Saul)

Jews of all ages (women and men) forced to scrub the streets of Vienna in humiliation as Nazi thugs supervise. (Photo courtesy of Eric Saul)

Vienna's Famous Hotel Sacher (Joy Kolitsky)

Sign on Jewish owned shop window in Vienna: "The Owner of this Business is a Jew." Jewish owned stores were eventually boycotted and eventually sold over for a fraction of their value to Aryan Austrians. (Photo courtesy of Eric Saul)

Nazi banner posted at the entrance to a town not far from Vienna. (Translation) "JEWS UNWANTED" (Photo courtesy of Eric Saul)

Bench in Vienna park with a sign. (Translation) "Only for Aryans" (non-Jews) (Photo courtesy of Eric Saul)

Chinese landscape, Dr. Ho's homeland (Joy Kolitsky)

Jewish Passport- Late 1930's into 1940's. Note Berta's forced middle name of "Sara" placed on every Jewish female's passport. A red "J" was also stamped on the front. (Image courtesy of the Schweider Family)

Jews leaving Austria after Nazi invasion and takeover. (Photo Courtesy of Eric Saul)

Jews lined up for visas in Vienna.

Jews line up for visas in another part of the city. (Image courtesy of Eric Saul)

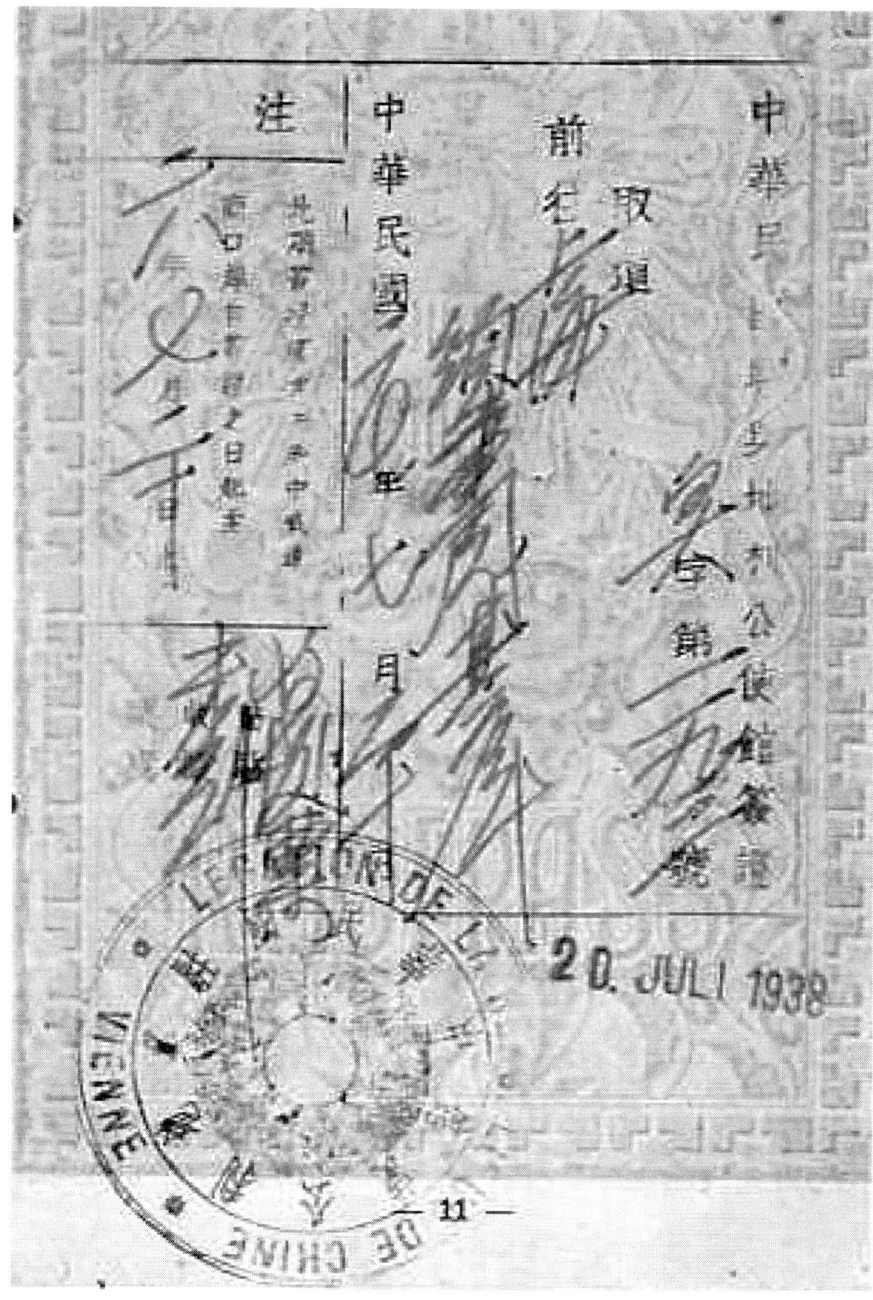

Exit visa administered and signed by Dr. Ho; a "golden ticket" out of the country to safety. (Photo courtesy of Eric Saul)

Viennese Jews lined up for visas out of the country to safety. .
(Photo courtesy of Eric Saul)

Official Viennese Passport Office with lines outside the building. Lines formed early in the morning and lasted until late in the day (Photo courtesy of Eric Saul)

Dr. Ho at his desk/typewriter. (Photo courtesy of Dr. Ho's family)

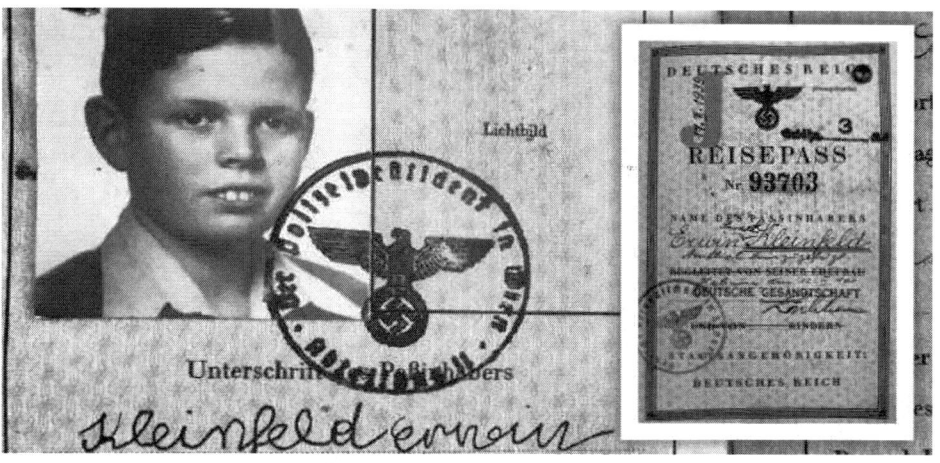

Young Jewish boy's passport: Erwin Israel Kleinfeld. Note the write-in of the middle name "Israel" required on all Jewish males' passports. (Photo courtesy of Eric Saul)

Jewish female's passport with middle name, "Sara". (Joy Kolitsky)

Jews aboard ship emigrating from Austria and to safety in Shanghai.

Ship has arrived in Port of Shanghai and is unloading cargo
and Austrian Jewish refugees.

Young Jewish child refugees are fed in the Shanghai Ghetto.

Shanghai Ghetto view of happy new arrivals.

Chinese Nationalist President Chiang Kai-Shek. (Joy Kolitsky)

President Chiang Kai-Shek with Dr. Ho in Taiwan after the war.
(Photo courtesy of Dr. Ho's family)

Dr. Ho back in China after the war before his new assignments.
(Photo courtesy of Dr. Ho's family)

Dr. Ho is dressed formally as ambassador from the Republic of China (Taiwan) to Egypt after World War II. He would thereafter serve as ambassador to Mexico, Bolivia and Columbia until his retirement in 1973. (Photo courtesy of Dr. Ho's family)

Dr. Ho (at right) with Nationalist Chinese officers and a British official. This photo was probably taken at the Nationalist capital of Chungking (The original capital, Nanking, had been destroyed by the Japanese). Fighting between the Nationalists and the Communists continued. This capital fell to the Communists in November of 1949, and in December the Nationalist government moved to Taipei on the island of Formosa (Photo courtesy of Dr. Ho's family)

Dr. Ho in retirement (1973) in San Francisco practicing his calligraphy. (Photo courtesy of Dr. Ho's family)

Dr. Ho's daughter, Man Li Ho at a United Nation's dedication ceremony for her father. (Photo courtesy of Dr. Ho's family)

Dr. Ho in the 1990s at age 96. He passed away in 1997. (Photo courtesy of Dr. Ho's family)

Feng Shan Ho Memorial plaque at the Shanghai Refugees Museum.

BIBLIOGRAPHY

Print Sources
Grebenschikoff, I. Betty, *Once My Name Was Sara*, Original Seven Publishing Co., Ventnor, NJ 1993.

Ho, Feng-Shan, *My Forty Years As a Diplomat,* Dorrance Publishing Co. Inc., Pittsburgh, PA, 1973.

Ho, Manli, et al., *Visas for Life*, Vancouver Holocaust Education Centre, Diplom*ats Who Saved Jews: Dr. Feng-Shan Ho. 1999.*

Zachor, The *Newsletter oft he Vancouver Holocaust Education Center*, Number 4, October 1999, pages 3-8, The VHEC, Vancouver, BC V5Z 2N7, 1999.

Internet Sources
Chang, Wayne, *Ho Feng-Shan: The Chinese Schindler Who Saved Thousands of Jews* , CNN, July 24, 2015.www.cnn.com.

Elis, Niv, Yad Vashem Taiwan Awards, *Ho Feng Shan China's Schindler" Presidential Honor*, Sept. 13, 2015.

Hall, Casey, The New York Times, Travel, *Jewish Life in Shanghai's Ghetto*, NY Times, 06/20/2012, http://nyt.ms?MevtZo

Jewish Virtual Library, /Righteous Among the Nations/Featured Stories/Feng-Shan Ho, China.

Katz Deborah, *Forgotten Holocaust Heroes: Dr. Ho Feng Shan, Little Known Chinese Savior of Jews*, jewqishpress.com, Sept. 27, 2018.

Paldiel, Mordechai, *China's Schindler: Dr. Feng Shan* Ho, Wong, Dr. James, Yad Vashem, People's Republic of China, Embassy, http:// chinbeseembassy.org

Saul, Eric, *Rescue in the Holocaust: Chronology of the Holocaust and Rescue in Austria, and Vienna: www.HolocaustRescue.org,*

Soloway Jewish Community Centre, Ottawa, Ontario, *Jews in China: An Enduring Friendship Between Two Ancient Cultures*

www.sen.parl.gc.ca/vpoy/english/Special_interests/speechesd/jewsin_china_ 021002.h,Oct. 2, 2002

Wong, Dr. James, Dr. Feng Shan Ho: Diplomat and Rescuer of Jews, McGill Research Project, http:// rwallenberg – int.org/Bulletin/Bul-2000/dr_Ho.htm